Starting a Pet Business: A Simple Guide to Success

Chapter 1: Introduction

Overview of the pet industry

The potential for growth and profitability

Chapter 2: Identifying Your Niche

Different types of pet businesses (e.g. pet grooming, pet daycare, pet retail)

Researching the market and competition

Chapter 3: Business Planning

Creating a business plan

Securing funding and managing finances

Chapter 4: Legal Considerations

Licenses, permits and insurance requirements

Employee laws and regulations

Chapter 5: Setting Up Your Location

Choosing a location and negotiating leases

Designing and outfitting your space

Chapter 6: Hiring and Managing Staff

Finding and hiring employees

Training and managing your team

Chapter 7: Marketing and Branding

Building your brand and creating a marketing plan

Utilizing digital marketing tools and social media

Chapter 8: Operations and Customer Service

Setting policies and procedures for daily operations

Providing exceptional customer service to retain clients

Chapter 9: Growing Your Business

Expanding services and offerings

Scaling and managing growth

Chapter 10: Conclusion

Reflection on the journey of starting a pet business

Tips for continued success and growth.

This book provides a comprehensive guide for entrepreneurs looking to start a pet-related business. It covers the important aspects of starting and running a successful business, from identifying your niche to growing and scaling your business.

CHAPTER 1: INTRODUCTION

Pet businesses have become increasingly popular over the past few years due to the growing trend of pet ownership and the increasing demand for pet-related services and products. The pet industry encompasses a wide range of businesses, including pet grooming, pet daycare, pet retail, pet food and supplies, and pet-related services such as pet training and pet sitting.

The potential for growth and profitability in the pet industry is significant, with the industry projected to continue its steady growth in the coming years. The growing trend of pet ownership and the increasing demand for high-quality pet products and services offer many opportunities for entrepreneurs to start and grow successful pet businesses.

In this book, we will guide you through the process of starting and running a successful pet business. From identifying your niche, to developing a solid business plan, to marketing and growing your business, this book provides practical advice and insights to help you achieve your goals and achieve success in the pet industry.

CHAPTER 2: IDENTIFYING YOUR NICHE

One of the first and most important steps in starting a pet business is to identify your niche. The pet industry encompasses a wide range of businesses, including pet grooming, pet daycare, pet retail, pet food and supplies, and pet-related services such as pet training and pet sitting.

Before you start your pet business, it is essential to research the market and understand the different types of pet businesses that exist. Consider your own interests, skills, and experience, and think about which type of pet business would best align with your strengths.

Once you have identified your niche, it is important to research the market and competition. This includes understanding the demand for pet-related services and products in your area, as well as identifying potential competitors and analyzing their strengths and weaknesses.

Market research can help you better understand the needs and preferences of your target customers and give you a competitive advantage. This information can also help you make informed decisions about your business, such as determining pricing, identifying potential suppliers, and developing a marketing strategy.

By thoroughly researching the market and competition, you can ensure that your pet business is well-positioned for success and profitability.

CHAPTER 3: BUSINESS PLANNING

Creating a comprehensive and effective business plan is an essential step in starting a successful pet business. A well-thought-out business plan not only helps you stay organized and focused, but it also makes it easier to secure funding and manage finances.

YOUR BUSINESS PLAN SHOULD INCLUDE THE FOLLOWING ELEMENTS:

Executive Summary: A brief overview of your pet business, including the products or services you will offer, your target market, and your goals.

Market Analysis: An analysis of the pet industry and market demand for your products or services. Include information on your target market, competition, and market trends.

Product or Service Offerings: A description of the products or services you will offer, including any unique features or benefits.

Marketing and Sales Strategy: A plan for how you will market your business and reach your target customers. Include information on pricing, advertising, and promotional activities.

Operations Plan: A description of how your business will operate, including information on location, hours of operation, staffing, and any equipment or supplies you will need.

Financial Projections: A detailed analysis of your expected expenses and revenue, including a projected income statement, balance sheet, and cash flow statement.

Funding Requirements: An estimate of the funds you will need to start and run your pet business, including any funding sources you have secured or plan to pursue.

By following this template and including all the necessary information, you can create a comprehensive and effective business plan that will help guide you in starting and running your pet business.

SECURING FUNDING AND MANAGING FINANCES

In addition to creating a business plan, it is important to secure adequate funding and effectively manage your finances. This may include seeking investment from friends and family, applying for business loans, or pursuing grants.

Once you have secured funding, it is crucial to create and adhere to a budget to ensure that your pet business remains financially stable. This may include tracking expenses, negotiating with suppliers, and monitoring cash flow.

By effectively managing your finances and staying on top of your budget, you can ensure that your pet business has the resources it needs to grow and succeed.

CHAPTER 4: LEGAL CONSIDERATIONS

Starting a pet business involves navigating a range of legal requirements and regulations. It is important to understand the necessary licenses and permits required for your business, as well as the laws and regulations that govern the employment of any staff.

OBTAINING NECESSARY LICENSES AND PERMITS

The licenses and permits required for your pet business will depend on a number of factors, including your location, type of business, and services offered. It is important to research the specific requirements for your area and obtain any necessary licenses and permits before starting your business.

This may include obtaining a business license, a sales tax permit, and any industry-specific licenses, such as a grooming or daycare license.

UNDERSTANDING EMPLOYEE LAWS AND REGULATIONS

If you plan to hire employees, it is important to understand the laws and regulations that govern the employment of staff. This includes minimum wage laws, overtime regulations, and laws related to employee benefits, such as health insurance and paid time off.

It is also important to understand laws related to hiring and firing, as well as equal employment opportunities and anti-discrimination laws.

By understanding the legal requirements for your pet business, you can ensure that you are operating within the law and protecting both your business and your employees.

CHAPTER 5: SETTING UP YOUR LOCATION

Choosing the right location and setting up your space is an important aspect of starting a successful pet business. Whether you are opening a retail store, a grooming salon, or a daycare facility, the location and design of your space will play a key role in attracting and retaining customers.

CHOOSING A LOCATION AND NEGOTIATING LEASES

When choosing a location for your pet business, consider factors such as accessibility, visibility, parking, and foot traffic. Research the local competition and market demand, and look for areas that are convenient for your target customers.

Once you have found a suitable location, it is important to negotiate a favorable lease agreement with the landlord. This may include negotiating rent, lease terms, and any additional expenses, such as property taxes and utilities.

DESIGNING AND OUTFITTING YOUR SPACE

The design and layout of your space can have a significant impact on the success of your pet business. Consider the needs of your customers and the services you will be offering, and design your space to meet those needs.

For example, if you are setting up a grooming salon, you will need to include bathing and grooming stations, as well as storage for equipment and supplies. If you are opening a daycare facility, you will need to create safe, comfortable play areas for the pets.

In addition to the functional aspects of your space, consider the overall look and feel of your business. Choose colors, furnishings, and decor that reflect your brand and appeal to your target customers.

By choosing the right location and designing a functional and attractive space, you can create a welcoming and comfortable environment for your customers and their pets.

CHAPTER 6: HIRING AND MANAGING STAFF

Hiring and managing a team of employees is an important aspect of running a successful pet business. Whether you are hiring a few employees or a large team, it is important to have a clear plan for recruiting, training, and managing your staff.

RECRUITING AND TRAINING EMPLOYEES

When recruiting employees, look for individuals who are passionate about pets and have the skills and experience necessary to succeed in your business. Consider conducting in-person or virtual interviews, as well as conducting background checks and reference checks.

Once you have hired your team, provide comprehensive training to ensure that your employees are equipped to deliver high-quality services to your customers. This may include training on specific skills, such as grooming or pet care, as well as training on customer service, sales, and communication.

EFFECTIVE MANAGEMENT TECHNIQUES FOR YOUR TEAM

As your business grows, it is important to implement effective management techniques to keep your team motivated and productive. Consider establishing clear goals and expectations for your employees, and provide regular feedback and coaching to help them succeed.

Consider using performance management tools, such as performance evaluations, to monitor the progress of your employees and identify areas for improvement. Encourage open and honest communication, and provide opportunities for growth and development within your organization.

By recruiting and training the right employees and implementing effective management techniques, you can build a strong, motivated, and productive team that is committed to the success of your pet business.

CHAPTER 7: MARKETING AND BRANDING

Marketing and branding are critical elements of building a successful pet business. To effectively reach and engage your target customers, it is important to develop a clear brand and marketing plan that communicates your unique value proposition and sets you apart from the competition.

BUILDING YOUR BRAND AND CREATING A MARKETING PLAN

To build your brand, start by identifying your target audience and understanding their needs, preferences, and pain points. Use this information to develop a unique value proposition that clearly communicates the benefits of your business and differentiates you from the competition.

Next, create a marketing plan that outlines your goals, budget, and strategies for reaching and engaging your target customers. Consider a range of marketing channels, including print and online advertising, direct mail, email marketing, and referral marketing.

UTILIZING DIGITAL MARKETING TOOLS AND SOCIAL MEDIA

Digital marketing tools and social media platforms can be powerful tools for building your brand and reaching your target customers. Consider creating a website and social media accounts for your pet business, and use these channels to share information about your products, services, and promotions.

Consider leveraging digital marketing tools, such as search engine optimization (SEO), pay-per-click (PPC) advertising, and email marketing, to reach and engage your target customers online. Use social media platforms, such as Facebook, Instagram, and Twitter, to build relationships with your customers and share information about your business in real-time.

By building your brand, creating a marketing plan, and utilizing digital marketing tools and social media, you can effectively reach and engage your target customers, grow your pet business, and achieve long-term success.

CHAPTER 8: OPERATIONS AND CUSTOMER SERVICE

Operations and customer service are critical components of running a successful pet business. To ensure that your business runs smoothly and effectively, it is important to establish clear policies and procedures, and to provide exceptional customer service to retain your clients.

ESTABLISHING POLICIES AND PROCEDURES

Establishing clear policies and procedures is an important step in ensuring that your pet business runs smoothly and effectively. Consider creating guidelines for operations, such as scheduling, customer service, and health and safety, and communicate these guidelines to your employees.

In addition, consider establishing clear protocols for handling customer inquiries and complaints, and for responding to emergencies. Ensure that your employees are trained on these policies and procedures, and are equipped to deliver high-quality services to your customers.

PROVIDING EXCEPTIONAL CUSTOMER SERVICE TO RETAIN CLIENTS

Providing exceptional customer service is critical to retaining your clients and growing your pet business. To provide high-quality customer service, start by setting clear expectations for your employees, and provide regular training and coaching to help them succeed.

Consider using customer relationship management (CRM) tools to track customer interactions and feedback, and use this information to identify areas for improvement. Respond to customer inquiries and complaints in a timely and professional manner, and look for opportunities to exceed their expectations and build long-term relationships.

By establishing clear policies and procedures, and providing exceptional customer service, you can ensure that your pet business runs smoothly, effectively, and successfully, and that your clients are satisfied and loyal.

CHAPTER 9: GROWING YOUR BUSINESS

As your pet business grows and matures, you will likely face new challenges and opportunities for growth. To successfully grow your business, it is important to expand your services and offerings, and to manage your growth effectively.

EXPANDING SERVICES AND OFFERINGS

Expanding your services and offerings is a key way to grow your pet business and reach new customers. Consider adding new products or services that complement your existing offerings, or exploring new markets or demographics that are under-served.

Conduct market research to understand the needs and preferences of your target customers, and use this information to develop new products and services that meet these needs. Consider collaborating with other pet businesses or industry experts to share resources, knowledge, and expertise, and to gain a competitive edge.

SCALING AND MANAGING GROWTH

Managing growth effectively is critical to the success of your pet business. As you expand your services and offerings, it is important to develop and implement effective systems and processes to manage your finances, operations, and customer service.

Consider implementing tools and technologies, such as project management software, customer relationship management (CRM) software, and financial management software, to automate and streamline your operations and processes. Hire and train additional staff as needed, and develop clear protocols for managing customer service and responding to emergencies.

By expanding your services and offerings, and managing your growth effectively, you can successfully grow your pet business, reach new customers, and achieve long-term success.

CHAPTER 10: CONCLUSION

Starting a pet business can be a challenging and rewarding journey, requiring dedication, hard work, and a commitment to excellence. In this book, we have explored key concepts and strategies for setting up and growing a successful pet business, from identifying your niche and creating a business plan, to expanding your services and offerings, and managing growth effectively.

REFLECTION ON THE JOURNEY OF STARTING A PET BUSINESS

Starting a pet business is not just about opening a shop or providing a service, but about building a community of customers who trust and appreciate the care and quality you provide. Reflect on your journey so far and the lessons you have learned, and celebrate your accomplishments along the way.

TIPS FOR CONTINUED SUCCESS AND GROWTH

TO CONTINUE YOUR JOURNEY OF SUCCESS AND GROWTH, CONSIDER THE FOLLOWING TIPS:

- Stay up to date on industry trends and developments, and be open to new ideas and strategies for growth.
- Foster strong relationships with your customers and employees, and encourage regular feedback and suggestions for improvement.
- Invest in your team by providing training and support, and recognize and reward their contributions to your success.
- Use technology and data to streamline operations and make informed decisions, and stay ahead of the curve with innovative products and services.
- Stay focused on your vision and mission, and never stop working to provide exceptional care and quality to your customers.

With these tips, you can continue to grow and succeed in the pet industry, and build a thriving pet business that provides happiness and comfort to pets and their families.

This comprehensive guide provides aspiring pet business owners with the knowledge and tools they need to start and grow a successful pet business. From identifying your niche and creating a business plan, to securing funding and managing finances, this book covers all the essential elements of starting and running a pet business.

With detailed chapters on legal considerations, setting up your location, hiring and managing staff, marketing and branding, operations and customer service, and growing your business, this guide is a comprehensive resource for anyone looking to enter the pet industry.